I0714360

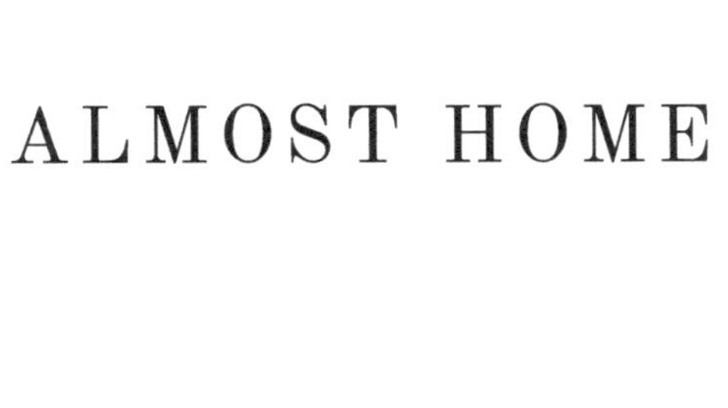

ALMOST HOME

ALMOST HOME

SELECTED POEMS

AARON CANCE

HOTHOUSE BOOKS Salt Lake City

Hothouse Books
9445 S. Union Square
Suite A
Sandy, UT 84070

"Almost Home" and "Testing the Water" first appeared in Southern Minnesota State University's **Bare Root Review**.

9781737456001 - Trade Paperback
9781737456018 - E-Book

First Printing, 2021

10 9 8 7 6 5 4 3 2

for Katherine & Viola

Contents

epiphany	1
the idea	2
Winter	4
Winter	6
Rupert	7
sitting in the dark	8
She	10
Lament for Kai Dionne	11
a peace; on sleep	12
one night out	14
Ode to Dewars	15
line applied in a disorderly manner	16
vigil	18
like flowers, again	20
a course in forgiveness	21

almost home	22
a peace; on the library	24
conditional	26
every december	27
youthful sins #5	28
falling down	30
poetry	32
curiosities of flight	33
germination	36
violin	37
teaching english	38
overture	41
one empty Tuesday	42
Wordsworth's Plight	44
Lavender	45
considering entropy	46
you're world	47
a taste of Ophelia	48
the finch	50
movement	51
in our fall	55

Tuesday, and possibly darker than Keats   56

landslide   57

rita hayworth   58

rabbits   60

the latest music   62

testing the water   63

asleep (voyage)   64

a grassland triptych   65

dandelion   68

writing (a new voyage)   69

sometimes it rains (when Tom sings)   72

aspen   73

suspension bridges   74

Wasatch trails   76

a lament for Icarus   77

can you find me?   78

rupert rattles   81

like a womb *   82

ode to coffee   84

A Few Notes   87
Gratitude   89

Preface

Until Dr. Richard Kirkwood put Mark Strand's "Eating Poetry" in front of me as an undergrad, I had gravely underestimated poetry. I had underestimated what it was, what it meant, what I could do with it, and, most importantly, what it would do for me. I had grown up on a farm in a small town in rural West Central Wisconsin, a place where very few people had any use for poetry. It wasn't, after all, paying for the groceries, feeding the livestock, mucking out pens, building fences, or putting hay up for anyone. Ten years after wandering out of my childhood home into the wider world, however, I found myself in an *Introduction to College Writing* course at the University of Wisconsin that would change almost everything that I thought I knew about poetry.

Up until that point, poetry felt like one of two things - good poetry and bad poetry. Unfortunately, bad poetry, to my young imagination, was a collection of cringe-worthy platitudes shoehorned into a hard and fast rhyme-scheme and good poetry was a dry, cryptic cipher, a language of the abstract understood only by the most erudite academics. Poetry, it seemed, was something that I would be destined to have no part of. I had no wish to partake in bad poetry and felt intellectually incapable of partaking of good poetry. The aforementioned English Professor, however, a kindly older gentleman who bore a striking resemblance to Santa Clause (don't think me unkind; he's made this claim repeatedly on his own) and had an affinity for bright orange, green, and yellow knee-high socks, begged to differ and turned Mark Strand's dogs loose on the entire class.

"Ink runs from the corner of my mouth," it begins, "There is no happiness like mine. I have been eating poetry." Poetry, it seemed, was actually wild and defiant. It was a little bit lawless and raw ("I get on my knees and lick her hand"). The form of the poem, it felt, barely contained the crackling energy of the language. Even at that young age, I instantly recognized the genius of the poem, and was electrified by it. Poetry wasn't some neat little plate of food that one ate with the knife in the right hand and the fork in the left, held at a forty-five degree angle, carefully trimming off bite sized pieces. No one would be watching to make sure my hands hovered approximately an inch off of the table. Poetry had a primordial intensity about it. It wasn't so much an art of hiding inside words, but one of charging them with meaning, to the extent that they felt about to break. Poetry wasn't over-intellectual (good poetry). It wasn't anti-intellectual (bad poetry). One went through the intellectual to reach poetry on the other side. It somehow invoked Albert Einstein's assertion that "if you can't explain it to a six-year-old, you don't understand it yourself." It was ridiculously complex and at the same time paradoxically simple.

So how, you might ask, would I describe poetry to a six-year-old? I would rely heavily on William Wordsworth, because of all the reading that I've done about poetry, and of all the poetry that I've taken the time to read, it is his notion of poetry that speaks to me the most. This might not be true for everyone, but you are all free to explain poetry in the way that it best makes sense to you. Quick flashback to Dr. Kirkwood, who once almost mystically uttered the philosophy, "that's the beauty of being a writer: if you don't like the reality that you live in, you can create a completely new one!" You can either find a philosophy of poetry that speaks to you, or you can make one up. I was lucky enough to find one. In his 1802 *Preface to Lyrical Ballads,* Wordsworth wrote that the "principal object, then," of the poetry "which I proposed to myself in these Poems was to chuse incidents and situations from common life, and to relate or describe them, throughout, as far as was possible, in a selection of language really used by men; and, at the same time, to throw over them a certain colouring of imagination, whereby ordinary things should be presented to the mind in an unusual way; and, further, and above all, to make these incidents and situations interesting by tracing in them, truly though not ostentatiously, the primary laws of our nature."

To the six year old, I would say, "a poet finds something really, really neat about plain and ordinary things and tells everyone about it. Sometimes, as people go through life, they feel like it can be pretty dull, until a poet shows them something interesting that they hadn't noticed before. By doing this, the poet makes this person's life more interesting, and sometimes even beautiful. A really good poet can write something that will make that person feel like life is really very special."

But let's leave our six-year-old behind and consider what poetry can do for adults. A number of months back, a friend of mine interviewed me for a feature he was working on for National Poetry Month. I remember that our discussion seemed to be focused on published poetry and the reader's experience with it. We also spoke about the process of having one's poetry published and the amount of effort that it took to become a professionally published poet. As someone who loves to write, I certainly have aspirations to professionally publish. Two of the pieces in this book were published by a small college in Minnesota. It didn't pay a thing, but the acceptance notification still had me over the moon. But (and our conversation transitioned into this idea) the acceptance and publication was a secondary reward. When you write something, I told my friend, you're doing nothing less than creating something from nothing - you're literally conjuring from thin air.

I have two manuscripts, I told him, novels, that are complete: one that I feel is altogether unpublishable and one that I think has commercial potential. However, when you say something like this to people who are your friends, they immediately tend to try to reassure you that perhaps you're being too critical of your own work, and that it just hasn't found the right home. I reassured him that, although I felt that the first novel would never make it into print, that I was nonetheless immensely proud of the thing that I had created. It was a two hundred and fifty page symphony of words (my own description, as it has a very unconventional narrative) with a beginning, a middle, and an end that had some truly lyrical and imaginative passages, and that meditated on what I thought were some significant philosophical questions. It was unpublishable, yes. But the day I completed my last revision and turned that final page down on top of the stacked pile of the manuscript, I felt a palpable sense of completion and my identity as a writer seemed to come into focus, my self-esteem blazed because I had actually seen to completion a writing project that had taken about ten years. In short, I had accomplished *something.* I had *created* something.

Everyone should write, I elaborated, and shared with him one of my favorite writing stories. In 2006, an English teacher at Xavier High School in New York gave her students an assignment to write a letter to their favorite authors, and they invited Kurt Vonnegut to visit their class. Although he declined in the most charming way, he also sent them an assignment. "Write a six line poem, about anything" he wrote, "Make it as good as you possibly can, but don't tell anyone what you're doing. Don't show it, or recite it, not even to your girlfriend or parents." And here's where Vonnegut arrived at the point. He closed out the note telling the Xavier students to then "tear it up into teeny-weeny pieces, and discard them into widely separated trash recepticals." He concluded, "You will find that you have already been gloriously rewarded for your poem. You have experienced becoming, learned a lot more about what's inside you, and you have made your soul grow."

Everyone should write stories and poetry and family histories and whatever else they'd like to write. Not to make money (that's a pretty high bar). Not for publication, or what we called in graduate school social capital. Everyone should write for the experience of writing. Everyone should have a chance to feel the sense of accomplishment that comes with creating something from nothing, to experience what it feels like when you take a deep dive into the well of your soul and return to the surface with something to share. Have I mentioned yet that I think everyone should write?

So that's where we've arrived. That's what this collection is. Here's an assortment of my poetry. Clearly I've disregarded Vonnegut's advice about throwing all of the poems away when I finished them, but the good Lord knows that I have thrown away plenty of them. Not everything works. Some pieces of writing never go anywhere, some poems never shine quite the way you hope they will, sometimes Chapter One isn't Chapter One, after all. But I've learned something from all of them. Each of them has made my life richer in some way - even the bad ones. So maybe go write something. Yes, you. Don't put it off until this weekend, or even tomorrow. I won't tell you what to write. Only you know what it will be, and what will be in it. But go do it. You might get a little frustrated, and you'll probably even throw some of it away. Maybe you'll throw it all away, and start over. But I can tell you one thing. If you stick with it, if you don't give up, if you keep writing, you'll be surprised at the way that it will light up the dark corners of your life.

epiphany

early it comes,
when the air is in a crisp dawn,
white cold,
running over the landscape
like escaping mice,
and, as they go tickling by
on scratchy twig feet,
epiphany smiles
like a cat in the corner
who has been waiting
and watching
all the while.

the idea

clings to the
power-line ropes that
dip under its relaxed weight.
charcoal eye
and cherry lip,
blood on the canvas;
the rabid crowd cheers
and I look at my idea
wondering
if I should

punch

it in the face again.
the balloon gloves
smell of old leather,
of india ink
and beg to sleep
as the idea buckles,

dropping to its words,
afraid.
but there is shame in violence
and guilt.
the crowd is deafening
but I can't finish this
today.

Winter

This morning
slipping and snowing
on the Chippewa River
footbridge
and the air
has a keen edge
an abrasive face
rubbing always
within its folds.

Minus eleven at
eleven of eight and
cold clings
wrist bare and
pervasive, slipping
silently inside
to cut the skin.

The Chippewa
fog filled and rolling
runs to greet my breath.
The river beneath
bound in a casing
of ice, crackling,
a frigid sheath.

Winter

On foot, exhaling,
frostbite clouds
clamor along behind
hungering
for latent warmth
wishing it would snow

Feet squeak and squeal
and the walker wears
his best crackling smile
crispy whiskers
wishing for the
pale shard
of the sun.

Rupert

Rupert
our smallest,
sings at one a.m.
when the lights go out
of his mind in the dark,
dancing and hopping,
hoping to be picked up,
rattling pleasantly,
perhaps at three a.m.
eating pine needles next
from the Christmas tree then
some sap in his fur
on his feet falling with
cups and plates
onto the kitchen floor,
running for the door,
perhaps around four.

sitting in the dark

four a.m.
and the lights change
in the intersection,
spreading emerald arms
that would wave you through
if you were there,
a glare in the mist;
then the crimson
silent signal splash
holds up hands to wait
and the motor vibrates
while municipal wiring hums
somewhere above, in the darnkess.

no one is here;
no one is coming,
and the only movement
is the vertical thrill
of the city lights
lancing the drowsy
dark cupola
above.

She

Have you found the lovely one?

Will she dance in fire for you,
and kiss controversy
on the lips?

Does she see you in her mind's eye
and feel you
on her fingertips?

Lament for Kai Dionne

lost child,
      dark boy,
in black water
fallen from the world
like a twig, slender,
snapped, trapped beneath
the pane of ice,
like Virgina Woolf's
apple vendor in the Thames,
downstream
from the dark portal,
passed through, new to the
other side now dreaming,
the small curled leaves
tangled in the
foliage of his hair,
unseen,
      untouched,
           unheard.

a peace; on sleep

I sleep
like I swim,
in silence,
slipping slowly
along the
river bed
of sheets,
arms spread widely,
watching
the distorted
ebullient light,
the aquatic life,
my wife,
snoring cats,
an oddly shaped
rocky pillow,
plunge, then,
to the depths,

to the ocean
floor of dreams
and distorted
nocturnal realities.

one night out

never should of
parked
behind that
rusty red pickup,
blocking
it in till
word got
to the Deuce
who come out
all full of piss
and whiskey,
with his thirty-eight,
and shot him
through
for the insult,
and went back
to finish his drink.

Ode to Dewars

(Concerning Food Offered to Idols)

shoot the scotch
and swallow,
feel the flame
rage the throat
and cup the hollow
belly, seeping upward,
spreading, dreaming
sleeping tendrils
tying it to my
head friendly heat.

the ice collapses
with disdain,
rattling vacuous prayers.

have one on me,
brother.

line applied in a
disorderly manner

the limb snapped off,
high above the ground,
dropped in the night,
and was caught
by other branches,
suspended,
tenuously trapped
and swinging
whenever the wind blew,
rubbing,
slipping,
and free again
free
fall to smash, unheard
in the darkness,

cleaving the plank fence
below
in two,
stabbing its limbs
into the wet grass,
waiting.

vigil

so damned hard
sleeping on the floor
rolled round in a
quilt, feather pillow
cradled in one arm,
baby in the other.

she won't sleep
in the bed,
not in her crib,
but only on
the smooth pine floor,
glossy with moonlight.

as a car breaks
the black horizon,

high beams suddenly
appear on the
bedroom wall, and
I watch the squares
of light linger, and
listen to the whispered
applause of the rolling tires on the asphalt,
the disconsolate rush
through the long,
dark country night,
along straight, lonely,
roads.

and, as the lit squares
begin to move,
edging into the corner,
then sliding silently
around the room,
her little girl snort
ripples the darkness,
heralding a return
to stillness.

like flowers, again

unkind imagination,
drift, and dream in darkness,
grow hungry and draw near
now, your face, touched,
palm to cheek,
fleshy frontier, waiting,
dreaming, like flowers,
of the first
shafts of dawn.

a course in forgiveness

the brittle
wafer breaks
like a bone
when I bite,
violence
with my teeth

my infidelities
are many,
and varied,
and the blood
an undeserved
aperitif.

almost home

a country boy can drown himself
by walking to the center of a field
at night
    undulating
           waves
                of
            oats,
   platinum in the moonlight.
thrust about rhythmically,
   circumambiently,
      in the fresh night wind.

thoughts play this way,
   and forgetting is easy
   under the indigo mythology of
                the sky,

forgetting reprobate
               physicality,
     drifting on stems and seeds,
             forgetting physicality,
                swooning,
                floating,

finally (betrayed) clutching instinctively
     at the raft of earth beneath his feet
             the bitter raft
             that will carry him to
             tomorrow
              and tomorrow
             and tomorrow
             and tomorrow.

a peace; on the library

outside the plate glass,
the city sits in a milky
glaze, and a river of taillights
streams down State Street in
a rush hour exodus.

streetlights twinkle and gleam
through wet pillows of foliage
and floodlights from the stadium,
a mile distant, shine up into
the dusk, a distant island of light.
a game tonight.

all the same, I'm warm and dry
sitting in the public library.
the book return cart trolls by
with one wobbly wheel knocking
to the beat of the rain,

its fingertips tapping
the roof overhead, when
a drunken transient wobbles
over to fall on the corner
of my table, looking

around, and under,
holding himself up,
relocating the self.
"Someone shtole my dufflebag."

I invite him into the poetry
reading, meet the poet,
and he groans
and trundles off,
going his solitary way.

conditional

he was now
hands on
in his love making,
now a participant
in an imperfect world.

she gave it to him,
told him to put it
in his mouth,
sweet and wet,
still twinkling
with stars
of the night's rain,

and he took it,
not because she asked,

but because
he wanted to.

every december

every december
counterfeit souls
wander
the stormy winter
roaming the perpetual whiteness,
dreaming of the captured crystals
that land in the hand,
transient flakes,
that live but a moment
and melt,
that die a trickling, watery death
in the time
of an arm.

youthful sins #5

thundering
around the carousel,
beneath a host of
barbed wire angels,
we, when children,
clutched their manes
and pulled their ears
without reservation
as the wooden horses
dipped and glided,
always on their way,
but moving
always in circles.

up and down
we drove them
and used them
until we realized
that the horses
had grown old,
that all the paint was chipping,
and they're discarded and burned
then,
and it's painful to abandon
the child like certainty
that the fixtures were all real.

falling down

every Saturday night
we'd stop to steal apples
from the Weston tree
on the corner,
that old pea green
Mustang purring
in the dark
behind us as
we bolted out
to snatch the fruit
from the outstretched
branches, burning
through the countryside,

everything black
but the sky.
we'd eat them, then,
in the dimly lit,
dashboard sanctuary,
smoking through
a perforated beer can,
snapping off
pieces of the
sweet flesh.

poetry

is the search,
is the wait
for the hot lash to strike,

is a violent shaking
of the imagination,
is the opening of dream-like wounds,
is the agitation of the cage,
of pulling the living coil tight,
and like a song on strings,
deliverance
from mediocrity.

one touch is all it takes
to calm the desolate soul,
one shaft of affectionate light
to remind the heart
that it is
a craving device.

curiosities of flight

proud, and round,
blood crested robin
flits to the ground,
bounds, hopping,
dragging worms from
the dew spangled lawn
in cold dawn
while Spring's blue
eggs sleep still,
nestled safely in soft
white pine boughs.

breathless barefoot boy
looks skyward, running
as four fighter planes
rip through the
soft cerulean sky over
the old farmhouse,
scream like demons
through the calm day,
and disappear pulling
thunder behind them
over the trees.

not at all like the
more familiar curiosity
of passenger planes
that arrive like apparitions,
on silent, sunny afternoons,
causing a silver glimmering,
pause to watch the
white streak stretch
across the newly
bifurcated expanse
of sky.

germination

flowers don't seek revenge,
as we do,
but would rather sink their stony teeth
into softer soils, biting to take root,
but with the tiniest taste of leaf,
with the slightest brush of a moist petal,
the strongest men readily bleed,
pressing,
resisting germination,
reckless hearts that are quick to die,
weeds are want to crust and brown,
but the truest unions
of stem and soil live on perpetually
in furious bloom.

violin

The bow is drawn across the strings,
    like fingers across a soul.
The past, the present, the future mix,
    to craft the sound of gold.
Whether furious dancing of the notes,
    or a tragic romantic seam,
The music is woven in a trance
    that enchants the listener's dream.
Into the night, the song moves on,
    in a haunting, fearful flight.
The artist, possessed, will not be stopped,
    save by dawn's first shafts of light

teaching english

lean back
in your stiff,
intolerable
vinyl chalkboard
chair,
looking at the ceiling,
gazing through the window,
walking around
anywhere outside
except the now, and
here's a little something
before we begin,
an anecdote,
a little pinch
to dull the pain.
please turn to page
forty-two,
and my work
will begin.

as I expound,
you may hear
toward the rear
of your head,
a drilling sound,
a suspicious scraping
of the bone,
and as we work
you may tense,
trying not to hear
how Huck and Tom,
how Jim, so dear,
made their way down
the river deep,
only grinding
the fine bone sand
of offensive words
between your teeth.

now rise,
rinse and clear,
clean the debris away,
wondering,
you are left wondering,
what, of this,
you'll need
for another day:
it is a debt of ideas.

and please,
despite your
numbness
and chalky demeanor,
accept my reassurances
that you will,
quite soon,
be feeling better.

overture

as the English wood
breathes in whispers,
naked hosts of trees
click their fingertips,
rocking against one another,
in a wooden lullabye.

the mossy soil snaps and pops,
saturated, and winter's paintbrush, daubed
spackles bright red berries
and rich green moss, swaying,
as this place plays its own symphony,
an overture of twigs and vines.

one empty Tuesday

driving alone
along the Mississippi
one empty Tuesday,
basking
in my relative smallness
beneath a pregnant pageant
of cumulus clouds,
drawn along
with the advance of
a legion of white-capped waves,
moving forward,
sliding south,
it occurred to me
that, in a canoe,
the current
would swallow me whole,
and that,
even as I settled,
languidly,

into the sweet black silt
of the bottom,
inhaling fish,
the river would continue
moving forward,
sliding south,
and the clouds would retain
every bit of
their robust dignity
paying no notice
to my misfortune.

Wordsworth's Plight

Someone's trampled Wordsworth,
once tall, bright in the garden,
The yellow trumpet in the air
has become bent, and trodden.

Stiff emerald spires that were his legs
are driven into the soil,
and worker's boots run to and fro,
oblivious to the trial.

Why walk upon this lovely thing?
Why tread without a care?
thrusting down your crushing weight
the poet cannot bear?

And now he lies there dying,
stem broken, leaves asunder,
The way that we all walk these days,
is something we should ponder.

Lavender

O' glorious wood, thy thick perfume,
In Spring dost thicken, with sumptuous bloom,
Thy air is heavy, with a wealth of scent,
Thy shafts, clothed in jade, to the heavens bent,
Tiny violet soldiers guard the earthen floor,
Sleepy blossoms burst, and their tint restore,
Thy sweet odour, would the richest course deter,
Through the breathing of thy life, of thy Lavender!

considering entropy

the simple warmth of the sun
is a petty pleasure
considering the energy
that i drop during the day,
dying simply and slowly
even as i learn how to live.
every groan in my bones
and squeak in my teeth
reminds me that the end is sure
and near now,
almost thirty or forty
years hence.
i am half finished.

you're world

i can trace
green and blue
geographic boundaries
around your fibrous land,
can see the hazy gleam
of sunlight stream
through your golden coils.
all of your
brilliant spheres
reflected,
the space between
land and sea,
the curious centered
wistful darkness,
and attraction,
cautiously calculating
the risk
of your gravitational
pull.

a taste of Ophelia

crumbling
brick buildings
hug the platform,
and the libidinous air
carries the lush taste of spring
in its grass green grasp.
the silence is broken
by breakneck fast trains
pounding through,
pressing the buildings
with their sudden appearance,
and songs of Ophelia
play about my heart,
like thunder,
rumbling
across moistened skies,
flopping, end over rocky end,
saturated exhilaration
of columbines and fennel.

the tender wind tosses
shelves of hair about
my eyes and face,
and the imposing noise
is suddenly covered
in the silence
of water,
and, as quickly as it had appeared,
the train shrinks on the horizon,
pulling the tracks along with it,
and I can still taste Ophelia
on my lips
and can still feel
her echoed song
in my fingertips.

the finch

the finch
lands in the crook
of my elbow,
little twig feet
on skin, and
flits
away.

I tell my father,
and he tells me
about the finch
he saw crushed
on the road,
feathers twitching
in the wind.

movement

as dusky figures pass
through Piccadilly,
submerged in languid lights
that dance and swing,
a lone guitarist plays
his acoustic,
and his large felt hat
lays, inverted, on the pavement,
jingling its cup.
the sidewalk is alive,
swinging its arms,
putting one foot in front of the other,
grabbing a paper bag
of roasted chestnuts
from a street vendor,
passing walking families,
passing the tube station
where Sylvester the Cat
plays jazz trumpet,
and, as the light fades

and the face of the city pales,
her tall iron lamps begin to
shine,
pushing the darkness up
away from the streets.

the air cools
as the day's exhaust dissipates,
and a blurry couple sit
with a half finished bottle
of Dolcetto,
hands entwined
in the garlic scented breast
of an Italian restaurant.
flags snap and crack
in the air over Trafalgar Square,
over parading pigeons
and bread throwers,
over an arguing couple,
and a criminal.
bubbly black taxi cabs
sit in stagnant traffic
carrying the loyal
home to their families,
while, in the offices,
the dedicated work late,
windows lit,
while young men and women
in clubs

move to twist to
disco is back
a sonic religion
dropping ecstasy
dancing to the pounding bass
and making love to
young men and women
in clubs.

the day's heat stays inside,
and the noise of passing cars
becomes a hush of breath.
ask any of the villagers
looking over the dark waters
living in cardboard homes,
a corrugated camp
on the bank of the Thames,
feet twitching, coughing,
waking to the new night,
beginning the necessary
search for food.
"Change, Sir?"
"Change for a cup of tea?"

at Gatwick, at Heathrow,
silver passenger jets
thunder up into the darkness
and float over the city
like shiny gods,

lights below reflected
in the mirror-like undercarriage,
in the play of clouds, shifting,
in the darkened windows,
faint faces look downward
from this swollen altitude,
look downward from
this safe place,
and, from this height,
it looks like there's no movement
at all
in London.

in our fall

i found my childhood again,
one rusty day in July,
when the rains fell hard,
and all the steel in the world
froze in place.
i wandered,
with the coarse and unruly
desires of the young,
from door to door, thumping
soiled,
seeking something holy
seeking something,
for i found
that i could no longer live,
even raw and formidable as i was,
only by means
of my favorite mechanisms.

Tuesday, and possibly darker than Keats

drawn forth by shameful lacrimation,
from your earthy womb,
you shift in your pot,

and, slowly raising your terracotta head,
gaze with blackened eyes,
shaggy sweet basil hair,
and cracks in your face,
we kiss.

there is soil on your breath,
sugary on your propped up materials,
in the folds of your decomposing dress,
and your flesh crumbles beneath my fingertips.

today, i am Tantalus, unsound.

landslide

waiting for you
on the sofa,
I felt the first
fragile notes
in the air, and
was drawn to
your bedroom
because you were
singing landslide
sweeter than Stevie
Nicks not knowing,
slowly crumbling,
I was watching
from the threshold,
suddenly loving you,
and feeling the
palpable, dreamlike terror
of the avalanche.

rita hayworth

and on the screen,
in a subdued and royal room,
in a palace,
a chamber,
an altar in bloom,
patrons find
the names of their gods
shining on metallic
silver cloth,
and rita hayworth,
being touched
by the gambler,
licks her lips
as her image flickers,
flashes,
a flower
innocent like a siren,
singing to passing ships,

all beauty,
grace,
and temptation,
forbidden fruit to pluck
pouting tight to the tree,
lids drooping,
shades drawn shut,
and nowhere
in particular
to go.

rabbits

the sky is
frozen black,
thick with stars,
and slender shadows
leap
and are caught
stealing
soundlessly
in the snowy
palm of the earth,
moving
between the
birdfeeder
and a patch of
icy ferns furtively,

stop
antenna ears
pivot alertly,
assessing,
waiting to see
if I am a killer
and, deciding not,
they slip away.

the latest music

having a baby
is like falling in love
for the very first time
all over again,
I think
as I press my nose
into her blanket,
into her tiny cotton jacket,
inhaling deeply,
deliberately drawing out
the scent that conjures
my new daughter,
her wee, round smiling face
and deliberate gaze
are the first pure song
I've heard in years.

testing the water

in the darkness
we walk across the ice,
a crackling
casement of death
daring drunk
northern wisconsin
boys bored in thick
flannel with bourbon
bottles

the frozen shelf
gunshot pops
it is a game
to see what life
will give us,
to see what we
can take away
without
indictment.

asleep (voyage)

I think (joke)
the difference (nexus)
between form (type) and function (read)
can be found just before bed (rest)
when breathing finds (balance)
equilibrium (stop)
a child (innocent)
in so many ways (imagine)
I (a child) used to dream (form)
(then) in my bed (form)
before I fell asleep (voyage)
now (exhausted)
I use my bed (function)
only for sleep (function)
and dreaming (function)
has become
incidental/accidental (coincidence)
(function)
(function)

a grassland triptych

1.
the hayloft is restive
and the last white ribbons of light
slip the slatboards leaving
lines across the floor, on the walls
chaff and dust float languidly
in the strips of sun, breathe, reach, and pass
cross over, and pound the basketball,
like a snare drum, on the floor,
pop pop pop
blow over spittle and sweat
sprays and drips perspire, respire,
aim, and jump like a diver
pass the ball and go
pop pop pop
touch a shoulder, an arm
twist, turn, and play
dance and dodge the
hoop rattles reality
and the ball springs away

rustling through the straw,
coming to rest against the
blue plastic cooler.

2.
rattle, and roll the red loft door open
to the pale twilight's reach
around the beam and hang half
into space, sitting on the edge
paddling the emptiness with boy feet
pop the tops off the bottles and flip
the caps rattling below blowing
wheat foam onto heaven like dew
drain the bottles vigorously
and the herd lows distant,
their peculiar meadow harmony
pop pop pop in the distance
draws stories of marijuana farmers
and cornfield killers, ragged green,
but God's truth it's kids in the gravel pit
shooting beer bottles for kicks
because in the grassland gloaming
we are all brothers
and have little but sovereignty
over time and space, surveying
kingdoms of fields, vast expanses
of crops, shifting in the wind.

3.
big falls and the rocks are broken
and bare feet freed from shoes
soft and sandy in the dark through
the foliage and the whole royal court,
a procession, moves through the trees,
swinging with drink down to the clearing,
where water thunders apocalypse in our ears,
falling over shelves of stone, luminous
in moonlight. It's like Trimalchio's feast, stripping
fast flashing naked in the gloom
bodies glow electric and, fresh with laughter,
rage impulsively into the stream
spraying diamond drops, swim and plash,
a quickening shiver, and we dive beneath
the surface licentiously then floating,
coasting, riding the currents, watching
the shaggy limbs of trees overhead,
and crawling onto the riverbed
as if for the very first time fire is made,
another two bottles of wine uncorked,
and the darkest hours of the night are passed
with the gratuitous talk of friendship.

dandelion

my reliable friend,

your round, warm face,
when you greeted me
in childhood,
was trustworthy
and constant.
and as i grew,
you held my wrist
with the simple,
unconditional friendship
you're known for,
and in your delicate old age,
with your full head of white hair,
you let go
a little at a time,
never clutching at
what's left behind
dandelion

writing (a new voyage)

what I saw (and thought)

I think (joke)
a contradiction
(you can't know what I think)
in the present tense (an utter impossibility)
in print (a trumpet declaration)
(inability) in print,
to (really) suggest
the present tense
I might think
and thought (and can)
in print, writing the form
of thinking (in writing)
while writing, then moving on
but print is trapped here (now)
in your hands
like a gunshot
that parts your hair,
you might shudder

to react (and may even hear the blast)
quasi-perceptually,
but you can never pull the trigger (here)
yourself.

what is (the space between us),
the difference between
whoever the hell it was that left
these words (here) for you to find
and your(self)?
how do you read your(self)
and how does your(self) read?
it's important.

the difference (nexus)
is the meeting and thinking,
the point at which
they connect (where black meets white)
the ink on the page,
and the intersection
of pages (at the binding
and, though men may
carry the casket into the hushed cemetery dusk,
you can never truly share my bereavement,
or feel the gnashing of my teeth
(but can only grieve behind your own eyes).

poetry doesn't suffer entropy

(though I might burn thin (eventually)
make your own (meaningful) story
as you will (form) and shape
(re)action.
waiting.

sometimes it rains
(when Tom sings)

unceasing, mist
drops directly down
cold outside the blinds,
and the poet
Waits to be heard,
hollow grumbling
from the cloth
of the wooden
box speakers speaking softly
about flowers and gravesites,
and the gravitational pull
of passing days
and passing cars
that push through
the perpetual mist
that drops directly down
outside.

aspen

there you are,
stout,
strong in the cold,
clean,
alpine air,
putting on
your best
bright yellow
friendly face
in the autumn,
unencumbered
by the
pitched scraping,
the blaring horns,
and grunting thunder
of traffic,
the rattling busses
that we call
a convenience.

suspension bridges

just before dawn
and in the long gallery
of bedewed sagebrush lies
an exhaustive series of
shimmering spider-webbed
suspension bridges
that sparkle like
jeweled pathways
whispering
with the delicacy of
an uttered word,
and, as the sun rises,
the invisible traps
appear in the light
and are avoided
like artwork.

there are those
who say they
all look the same,
that they sound
the same to some
like a string quartet,
but a longer look
with an eye
trained for
forbearance
reveals a blast
of passion,
the creative impulse
evident in even
the smallest
living creatures.

Wasatch trails

passing between patches
of shimmering
aspen shade
and weighty sunlight,
stony Wasatch trails
wind about
the desiccated hillside,
crusty with the crisp scent
and fresh death
of autumn.

the suserrating leaves
and rattling brush
tell tales of fragile
and calculated decay,
but a battalion of spruce
stand at attention,
overseeing
the laws in place.

a lament for Icarus

finally at rest, Icarus.
i saw you sail free,
set your heading high,
for the clouds,
never suspecting
that your wings of wax
weren't made to last.
fly fast
lest some
earthbound archer
take envious aim
at your ambition,
ego bought back
with your bloody feathers.

now you float
finally free
of earthly live
captivity.

can you find me?

here   in this place   while you stand or sit
in your space   in your own space
     air hot with a hundred thousand   voices
chanting   while bodies sweat
     and sway to the   dreamy drum beat

     dreaming a darkened
sky of steel   and concrete
     sky architecture
     ventilation architecture
     breathe together deeply   and sing
          together
     the hundred thousand   voices
high and low

band and stage climb
     the space above   transcend
together   beyond the purchase price
     beyond the t-shirts

                        climbing   the spiral
of sound
                together
            sing together
can you find me

                                                        in the dark?

                                                    do you know
me?
                are you the blonde   with big blue eyes
                        blonde who kissed me
hard and drunk and,
                like a lamb   I opened my mouth
you tossed it in, small and white   and
                                            we laced ourselves
together like fingers
                    under clothing   eyes closed
        shifting from foot   to foot   to foot
to slowly drift

        voices together like
        a legion of angels
you, too,   riding the river,   the surface of the song,
dipping and gliding, voices
                calling
your voice vibrating, body
        vibrating   from the sound
it made.   I can feel you
sing.
do you know who I am?   one voice
in the throng loud and strong, but   anonymous
weaving behind words and   searching.

rupert rattles

rupert rattles
on the bed
loudly
roundly,
and soft
in the middle now,
made lazy
in aging,
his
hazy little
head
in bed now
sleeping
the whole
night through.

like a womb *

i walked up behind her
her scent enchanted me
her hair was soft and sweet
reaching around her waist
pulling her close, tight
i made my way through her hair
and whispered
i love you
the room is warm and dark
everything is close

he approached from behind
i could feel his presence
he pushed his face into my hair
his strong arms collecting me
drawing me in
he leaned around, over my shoulder
breath, hot on my cheek
i love you
the room is dark
and warm

like a womb.

Written to be performed aloud by two alternating voices. Reader one begins. When he lands on the last word of the line, reader two is reading the first word of the companion line simultaneously. When reader two arrives at the final word of the first line, reader one does the same with the first word of the second line, and so on until they reach "like a womb" which is read together.

ode to coffee

on the cusp
of cold days
you rise
my rich
bitter
greeting of
day break
black

in the
porcelain
morning
you trickle
to steam
sleep farewell
and not
turn back.

A Few Notes

The expression "there is nothing new under the sun" is frequently invoked, but is often incorrectly attributed to Shakespeare. My best guess is that it somehow gets conflated with his Sonnet 130, which begins "My mistress's eyes are nothing like the sun." The expression actually comes from Ecclesiastes 1:9 in *The Holy Bible*, which reads "What has been is what will be / and what has been done is what will be done / and there is nothing new under the sun." Nothing is ever really new; all writers, artists, musicians, filmmakers, etc. find their vision in what others have done before them. Some of these little poems owe a debt of gratitude to other, far greater, works.

Lament for Kai Dionne was inspired by Melanie Rae Thon's stunning novel, *The Voice of the River*.

one night out, unfortunately, was inspired by a real incident that took place at a backwoods roadhouse when I was young, and it stuck with me.

Violin was inspired by, and written for, a young Japanese student named Luke Ho, out of gratitude both for a 1 a.m. concert in Harlaxton Manor's Great Hall while we lived there, and for his seemingly endless patience helping me as I fumbled through three months of introductory Kung Fu. Luke taught me that, with enough discipline, my whole life could actually be a work of art.

Although most of the pieces in this book are inspired by noteworthy moments, *taste of Ophelia* was also heavily fueled by Natalie Merchant's song "Ophelia," that both provided the backdrop in the moment and was used to recapture the spirit of it afterward during revisions.

Tuesday, and possibly darker than Keats was directly inspired by the poem *Isabella, or The Pot of Basil* by John Keats, which, in turn, was inspired by a story from Boccaccio's *The Decameron*.

rita hayworth was inspired by the film *Gilda*

sometimes it rains (when Tom sings) was inspired by his song *Flower's Grave* on the album *Alice*.

a lament for Icarus was inspired by the breathtaking painting of the same title by Herbert Draper in The Tate Gallery.

Gratitude

My life has been made more meaningful by knowing the people on this page, and they all deserve acknowledgement and love for a number of different reasons. I'm grateful to

- my family of readers. to my parents who always had books around the house while we were growing up, even when the furniture wasn't as nice as it is now. Their bookshelves are where I saw my first copies of *Do Androids Dream of Electric Sheep*, *Moby Dick*, *The Pearl* , and I could go on and on, because they had a lot of bookshelves.

- the family of readers that I married into, for loving me like I was their own. No normal person owns as many books as I do, and I'm constantly grateful that you've chosen to overlook this.

- to my wonderful reading wife. I knew you were the right one when we could silently share a couch reading for hours. I'm still grateful for whatever it was that led you into Kirkwood's Chaucer class!

- to my beautiful daughter, who is at the beginning of her reading life. Here's to the many and various bookish adventures ahead of you. I hope you find the same type of wonderful gatekeepers and riverguides to lead you to and through these worlds that I did.

- to Rick Wulterkins, for showing me the way to *Firestarter, Cat's Cradle, Lord of the Flies, Romeo and Juliet, Macbeth, Antigone,* and others. Furthermore, your giving me extra-credit for every piece of creative writing that I produced both taught me that I had value, my writing had value, and helped me pass your class. You get extra credit for the rest of my life.

- to Richard Kirkwood, who helped me realize that poetry was for everyone, and then walked me through Chaucer's *The Canterbury Tales* in modern verse, and then a second time in the original Middle English.

- to Dr. Carol Fairbanks, for introducing me to the beauty of both Black Literature and Japanese Literature. We went on a voyage that included Ralph Ellison's *Invisible Man,* my first Toni Morrison book, *Jazz,* Langston Hughes, Paul Lawrence Dunbar, Jean Toomer, and also writers like Kobo Abe, Yasunari Kawabata, Fumiko Enchi and others. These two bodies of work continued to nurture and sustain me decades after your two classes came to an end.

- to Barry Weller, who helped me open up Milton's *Paradise Lost* and William Wordsworth's *The Prelude,* as well as introducing me to the incomparable work *The Faerie Queene* by Edmund Spenser.

- to Scott Black, who, by way of two different courses, walked me through the development of the novel as a form - from Apuleius, Heliodorus, and Petronius to Cervantes, to Henry Fielding, Daniel Defoe, Jonathan Swift, Laurence Sterne, Samuel Richardson, all the way up to the advent of the Gothic novel.

- to Kathryn Bond Stockton, whose Literary Theory class discussions always left my brain ablaze for hours afterward.

- to the members of the Japanese Literature Book Club, who were a voracious group of readers. After reading Japanese writers for two years, the same group read Russian Literature for a year and then French authors for yet another year. You guys have a serious hunger for good books!

- to all the readers that I've come into contact with at Barnes & Noble, Ken Sanders Rare Books, The King's English, and The Printed Garden who have ever recommended an author or a book that you have loved. This is how the best books stay alive, regardless of their box-office numbers!

- last, but certainly not least, to the friends and colleagues who assisted with this book. A big thank you to Bill Dunford for kindly letting me use one of your spectacular images on the cover of this book. Special thanks to all the early readers of my poems for your ongoing support and criticism, and I'm particularly grateful to Utah poets Nancy Takacs, Nathan Hauke, and Alex Caldiero for reading through the pieces that made it into this book, and for the terrific endorsements!

Aaron Cance has a B.A. in English Literature from the University of Wisconsin and a M.A. in British and American Literature from the University of Utah. He and his family own a modest, but well curated, bookstore in the City of Sandy called The Printed Garden, and live with three cats of questionable disposition in Salt Lake City.